ETIQUETTE

FOR

LITTLE FOLKS.

SUSIE SUNBEAM'S SERIES.

BOSTON:
G. W. COTTRELL, PUBLISHER.
36 Cornhill.

Entered according to Act of Congress, in the year 1856,

BY J. Q. PREBLE,

In the Clerk's Office of the District Court of the United States for the Southern District of New-York.

Stereotyped by
NESMITH & TEALL,
29 Beekman Street.

ETIQUETTE

FOR

LITTLE FOLKS.

RULES FOR GOOD BEHAVIOR AT HOME.

Never enter the house with your hat on, and always bow to any strangers you may meet at home.

If you pass by your parents at any place, where you see them, either by themselves or with company, always bow to them.

If you wish to speak to your parents, and see them engaged in discourse with company, draw back, and leave your business till afterwards; but if it is really necessary to speak to them, be sure to whisper.

Never speak to your parents without some title of respect, as Sir, Madam, &c.

Dispute not, nor delay to obey your parents' commands.

Go not out of doors without your parents' leave, and be sure to return by the limited time.

Never grumble, or show discontent at any thing your parents appoint, speak or do.

If any command or errand is given you to perform, do it with alacrity.

Bear with meekness and patience, and without murmuring or sullenness, your parents' reproofs or corrections, even if it should sometimes happen that they are undeserved.

Never make faces or contortions, nor grimaces, while any one is giving you commands.

Never take another's chair, if it be vacated for a short time; it is impolite.

Never quarrel with your brothers and sisters, but live in peace and amity.

Use respectful and courteous language towards all the domestics. Never be domineering nor insulting, for it is the mark of an ignorant and purse-proud child.

AT TABLE

Come not to table without having your hands and face washed, and your hair combed.

Sit not down until your elders are seated. It is unbecoming to take your place first.

Offer not to carve for yourself, or to take anything, even though it be something you much desire.

Ask not for anything, but tarry till it be offered to you.

Find no fault with anything that is given you.

When you are helped, be not the first to eat.

Speak not at table. If others are discoursing, meddle not with the matter; but be silent, except when spoken to.

If you wish anything from the servants, call them softly.

Eat not too fast, nor with greedy behavior.

Eat not too much, but moderately.

Eat not so slowly as to make others wait for you.

Make not a noise with your tongue, mouth, lips, or breath, in eating or drinking.

Be sure never to speak with food in your mouth.

Endeavor so to eat, that

none may see your food while chewing.

Stare not in the face of any one, especially your elders, at the table.

Lean not your elbow on the table, nor on the chair back.

Spit not, cough not, nor blow your nose at the table, if it can be avoided; but if it be necessary, do it aside, and without noise.

Stuff not your mouth so much as to fill your cheeks. Be content with small mouthfuls.

Blow not your food when too hot, but wait with patience till it becomes cool.

Smell not of your food; turn not the other side of it upward to view it on your plate.

Spit not forth anything that is not convenient to be swallowed, such as the stones of plums, cherries, or the like; but with your left hand, neatly move them to the side of your plate.

Fix not your eye upon the plate of another, nor upon the food on the table.

Lift not up your eyes, nor roll them about while you are drinking.

Bend your body a little

downward to your plate, when you move anything that is carried to your mouth.

Look not earnestly on any one that is eating.

Gnaw not bones at the table, but clear them with your knife, (unless very small) and hold them not with the whole hand, but with two fingers.

Drink not with anything in your mouth.

Before and after you drink, wipe your mouth with your napkin.

Never pick your teeth at table.

Never drink till you have quite emptied your mouth, and do not drink often.

Enter not in company without a bow.

Be careful not to turn your back to any, but place yourself so that none will be behind you.

Lean not on the chair of a superior, standing behind him.

Touch not, nor look upon the books or writing of another, unless the owner invite or desire it.

Come not near when another reads a letter, or other paper.

Let your countenance be moderately cheerful, neither laughing nor frowning.

To look upon one in company, and immediately after whisper to another, is unmannerly.

Whisper not in company. Be not froward and fretful among your equals, but gentle and affable.

If you cannot avoid gaping,

shut your mouth, with your hand or handkerchief before it, turning the face aside.

AMONG OTHER CHILDREN.

As near as may be, converse not with any but those that are good, sober, and virtuous: "Evil communications corrupt good manners."

Reprove your companions as often as there shall be occasion, for wicked actions or indecent expressions.

Be willing to take those

words or actions as jesting, which you have reason to believe were designed as such.

If your companion be a little too sarcastic in speaking, strive not to take notice of it, or be moved at all by it.

Abuse him not, either by word or deed.

Deal justly among those who are your equals, as solicitously as if you were a man with men, and about business of higher importance.

Be not selfish altogether, but kind, free, and generous to others.

Avoid sinful and unlawful recreations, and all such as prejudice the welfare of body or mind.

Scorn not, nor laugh at any because of their infirmities; nor affix to any one a vexing title of contempt and reproach; but pity such as are so visited, and be glad that you are otherwise distinguished and favored.

IN SCHOOL

Bow at entering, especially if the teacher be present.

Walk quietly to your own seat, and move not from one place to another till school time be over.

If your teacher be conversing with a stranger, stare not at them, nor listen to their talk.

Interrupt not your teacher while a stranger or visitor is with him, but defer any question or request till he be at leisure.

If your teacher speak to you, rise up and bow, making your answer standing.

If a stranger speak to you in school, stand up and answer, with the same respect and ceremony, both of word and gesture, as if you were speaking to your teacher.

Make not haste out of school, but soberly retire when your turn comes, without hurry or noise.

Go not rudely home through the streets. Stand not talking with boys who delay you; but go quietly home, and with all convenient speed.

AT CHURCH.

Walk quietly and soberly to the pew; run not, nor go playing.

Sit where you are directed by your parents.

Change not seats, but continue in the place where you are desired.

Talk not in church. Fix your eye upon the minister;

let it not wildly wander to gaze on any person or thing.

Attend diligently to the words of the minister. Pray with him when he prays, at least in your heart; and while he is preaching, listen attentively, that you may remember. Be not hasty to run out of the church after the worship is ended, as if you were weary of being there.

Walk decently and soberly home, without haste or playfulness, thinking upon what you have been hearing.

Always remember to be punctual at church. Never, if it can possibly be avoided, disturb the services by coming in after they have commenced.

IN THE STREET

Walk quietly and unobtrusively in the street, neither singing, whistling, or shouting.

Affront none, especially your elders, by word or deed.

Jeer not at any person, whatever.

Always give the right hand to your superiors, (by superiors, I do not mean so much in regard to birth, as age, merit, and the light in which they are regarded by the world,) when you either meet or walk with them; and mind also to give them the wall, in meeting or walking with them; for that is the upper hand, though in walking your superior should then be at your left hand.

But when three persons walk together, the middle place is

the most honorable; and a son may walk at his father's right hand, while his younger brother walks at his left.

Give your superiors place to pass before you, in any narrow place where two persons cannot pass at once.

If you go with your parents, teacher, or any superior, go not playfully through the streets.

Pay your respects to all you meet, of your acquaintance or friends.

It is impolite to stare at every unusual person or thing which you may see in the street, or to use any improper postures, either of head, hands, feet, or body.

TO YOUR PARENTS.

Children, these are the most essential of those rules of behavior, the observance of which will deliver you from the disgraceful titles of sordid and clownish, and entail upon you the honor of being called well-bred children; for there is scarcely a sadder sight, than a clownish and unmannerly child. Avoid, therefore, with the greatest diligence, so vile an ignominy.

Be humble, submissive, and obedient to those who have a just claim to your subjection, by nature and providence: such are parents, masters, or tutors, whose commands and laws have no other tendency than your truest good. Be always obsequious and respectful, never bold insolent, or saucy, either in words or gestures.

Let your body be on every occasion, pliable, and ready to manifest, in due and becoming ceremonies, the inward reverence you bear towards those above you.

By these means, by timely and early accustoming yourselves to a sweet and spontaneous obedience in your youthful stations and relations, your minds being habituated to that which is so indispensably your duty, the task of obedience in farther relations will be performed with greater ease and pleasure; and when you arrive at manhood, there will remain in your well-managed minds no presumptuous folly, that may tempt you to be other than faithful and good citizens.

TO SUPERIORS

Among superiors, speak not till you are spoken to, or are asked to speak.

Hold not your hand, nor anything else before your mouth when you speak. Come not very near the one you speak to.

If your superior speak to you while you sit, stand up before you give an answer.

Speak not very loud, nor too low. Answer not one who is speaking to you, till he is done.

Strive not with your superiors, in argument or discourse; but easily submit your opinion to their assertions.

If your superior speak anything wherein you know he is mistaken, correct not, nor contradict him, nor laugh at the hearing of it; but pass over the error, without notice or interruption.

Speak not, without Sir, or some other title of respect, which is due to him to whom you speak.

Mention not frivolous or little things among grave persons or superiors.

If your superior hesitate in his words, pretend not to help him out.

Come not very near to two that are whispering, neither ask what they converse upon.

When your parent or master speaks to any person, speak not, nor hearken to them.

If immodest words be used in your hearing, smile not, but settle your countenance, as if you did not hear it.

Boast not in discourse of your own wit or doings.

If your superior be relating a story, say not, "I have heard it before," but attend to it as if it were altogether new to you. Seem not to question the truth of it. If he tell it not right, suggest not, nor endeavor to help him out, or add to his relation.

Beware how you utter anything hard to be believed.

Interrupt no one in speaking, though he be your intimate.

Coming into company when any topic is being discussed, ask not what was the preceding conversation, but listen to the remainder.

Laugh not in, or at, your own story, wit or jest.

Speaking of any distant person, it is rude and unmannerly to point at him.

Be not over earnest in talking, to justify your own words.

Let your words be modest, about those things which concern only yourself.

Repeat not the words of a superior, who asks you a question, or talks with you.

TO EQUALS.

Be kind, pleasant, and loving, not cross, nor churlish, to your equals; and in thus behaving yourselves, all persons will naturally desire your familiar acquaintance; every one will be ready and willing, upon opportunity, to assist you.

Your friends will be then all those who know you, and observe the excellence and sweetness of your deportment. This practice, also, by inducing a habit of obliging, will fit you for converse and society, and facili tate and assist your dealing with men in riper years.

TO INFERIORS.

Be meek, courteous, and affable to your inferiors; not proud nor scornful. To be courteous, even to the lowest, is a true index of a great and generous mind. But the insulting and scornful one, who has been himself originally low, ignoble, or beggarly, makes himself ridiculous to his equals, and by his inferiors is repaid with scorn and hatred.

RECOGNITIONS.

A gentleman, on meeting a lady of his acquaintance in the street, or elsewhere, should not presume to bow to her, till she has first recognised him; or she may feel compelled to notice him, when she would not choose to do so otherwise.

A gentleman should never recognise a lady, to whom he has never been presented, at a ball or evening party, and should pass her as a stranger, unless she chooses to recognise him, when he should, as in all other cases, return the salute.

A very young person should wait to be recognised by one more advanced in age.

INTRODUCTIONS.

On giving introductions, always present a gentleman to a lady, save when a lady enters a room where several persons are assembled, when the lady is presented. Very young persons should be presented to older ones; and we should always present individuals TO those persons to whom we owe particular respect, on account of age, station, &c.

It is in good taste to present both parties, merely inverting the order of the names.

COMPLIMENTARY CARDS AND NOTES.

Miss Foster presents her compliments to Miss Edwards, and requests the honor of her company at a Tea-party, on Wednesday afternoon.

16 Arch street.

Tuesday noon.

Miss Edwards presents her respects to Miss Foster, and

accepts her kind invitation with pleasure.

30 Chestnut street.
Tuesday noon.

Miss E. presents her respects to Miss F., and regrets that a pre-engagement prevents her acceptance of her polite invitation.

William Harris presents his

respectful compliments to Miss Brown, and trusts she has experienced no ill consequences from her last evening's fatigue at the assembly.

Miss Brown finds herself greatly obliged by Mr. Harris' kind inquiries, and is happy to inform him she is perfectly well.

Miss Brown is greatly obliged by Mr. Harris' kind inquiry, and is sorry to say that she suffers under a severe cold, in consequence of last evening's amusement.

Mr. W. presents his compliments to Mr. S., and hopes, if Mr. S. is disengaged, that he will dine with him on Monday next, at half-past three o'clock.

Mr. S. presents his respects to Mr. W., and will avail himself of his kind invitation with pleasure.

Mr. S. regrets that indisposition will prevent him the honor of dining with Mr. W on Monday next.

Miss Dudley's compliments to Mrs. Windsor, and will be

obliged by her company to dinner on Thursday next, at three o'clock.

Mrs. Johnson returns her best respects to Mr. Wilson, and is greatly indebted to him for his obliging present.

Mr. and Mrs. Bristow present their compliments to Mrs. Truman, and hope for the pleasure of her company on Thursday evening next, to tea.

Mr. and Mrs. Truman are greatly obliged by Mr. and Mrs. Bristow's kind invitation, and will do themselves the honor of waiting upon them.

Mr. and Mrs. Truman are exceedingly sorry that a pre-engagement will prevent them from accepting Mr. and Mrs. Bristow's kind invitation.

DINNER PARTIES.

Whenever dinners are given to invited guests, civility requires that an early answer should be returned; for the proper wording of such answers, I refer you to the Notes of Invitation, where full directions are given. An acceptance, in such a case, should be as binding as a prommissory note; and no light cause should ever be allowed to prevent your fiulfilling your engagement. Want of punctuality at a dinner party, is an affront to the whole company, as well as to the gentleman and lady of the house.

A ceremonious dinner requires that the company be well and handsomely dressed, though not in such gay attire as is usually worn at a ball or evening party.

Arrived at the place, and disrobed of your cloak, let your gloves be on, and with erect form and firm step, enter the parlor. Look towards the lady of the house, and walk up at once to her, not turning to the right or the left, or noticing any one, until you have made your bow to her, and to the host. Then you may turn off towards the young people, and take a seat among them, with that agreeable expression of sympathy on your face, which encourages conversation.

On entering the dining-room, you must use your eyes to discover which part of the table is considered the most honorable. Try to seat yourself among the least important portion of the company, unless desired by the lady or gentleman of the house to take a particular seat.

When fairly seated in the right place, spread your napkin in your lap to protect your dress from accident; take off your gloves, and put them in your lap, under your napkin.

When you send your plate for anything, whether by the

hand of a servant or friend, take off the knife and fork, and lay them down on the cloth, supporting the ends on your bread, or hold them in your hand in a horizontal position.

After dinner, you are expected to take leave more generally and sociably, than after any other kind of party, except it be a small supper party.

GOING INTO COMPANY.

A young person ought to be able to go into a room, and address the company, without the least embarrassment.

Ignorance and vice are the only things of which we need be ashamed. Avoid these, and you may go into what company you will.

A modest assurance in every part of life, is the most advantageous qualification we can possibly acquire.

GOOD BREEDING.

To show the politeness of a true gentleman, you must be quick to observe four things:

1. What your place is.
2. What is due to every person.

3. How to do what is proper in an agreeable manner.

4. How to make yourself acceptable to others, in person, manners, and conversation.

You can be as polite to the boot-black as to the President. This is done, not by an air of condescension, but by treating him as a man, according to his place. Render him his due, and he will be likely to render you yours.

The same person who is overbearing to his inferiors, is likely to show a cringing servility to his superiors. Both faults are marks of a mean and groveling mind. Maintain your self-respect, if you would enjoy the respect of others.

Cherish that delicacy of sentiment, that quick sympathy

with others, that nice sense of justice which will make you as regardful of their feelings as of their more substantial rights, and you will not fail to be polite. Without the sentiments of a gentleman, you may know all the rules of politeness, and be scrupulously observant of all the external forms of good breeding, and yet never be a gentleman.

In short, to be a true gentleman, you must be generous and noble, as well as just and courteous. You must be scrupulously careful to be—Pure in body, pure in manners, pure in morals, and pure in heart.

Follow fashion moderately, if you would follow it gracefully. Never rely on dress to make you a gentleman. It is as flimsy a disguise as the lion's skin was to the ass; his braying betraying him, and his unsuitable attire only made him appear the more ridiculous.

A good enunciation is a distinctive mark of good breeding. Speak your words plainly and distinctly, and in a moderate tone of voice. Pronounce words in the manner that is used by the best bred persons, but not affectedly, or with a strained precision. Avoid all vulgar or inaccurate vowel sounds, as keow, ile, soit, for cow, oil, sight. Do not slip or smother your consonants, as gen'lm'n for gentleman, mornin' for morning &c.

CLEANLINESS.

No one can please in company, however graceful his air, unless he be clean and neat in his person.

He who is not thoroughly clean in his person, will be offensive to all with whom he converses. A particular regard to the cleanliness of your mouth, teeth, hands, and nails, is but common decency.

A foul mouth and unclean hands, are certain marks of vulgarity; the first is the cause of an offensive breath, which nobody can endure, and the last is declarative of dirty work, and disgraceful negligence to remove the filth. One may always know a gentleman by the state of his hands and nails.

The flesh at the roots should be kept back, so as to show the semicircles at the bottom of the nails; the edges of the nails should never be cut down below the ends of the fingers, nor should they be suffered to grow longer than the fingers.

For black and dirty teeth, where they are sound, there can be no excuse. They are the mark of a lazy, vulgar fellow. Let me entreat you to form the habit of brushing your teeth, every night before you sleep.

Now, clean garments and a clean person, are as necessary to health, as to prevent giving offence to other people. It is a maxim with me, which I have lived to see verified, that he who is negligent at twenty years of age, will be a sloven at forty, and intolerable at fifty.

GRACEFULNESS.

Be graceful in your manners. The different effects of the same thing, said or done, when accompanied or deserted by graceful manners, is almost inconceivable. They prepare the way to the heart. From your own observations, reflect what a disagreeable impression, an awkward address, a slovenly figure, an ungraceful manner of speaking, whether fluttering, or drawling, &c., make upon you, at first sight, in a stranger, and how they prejudice you against them.

MODESTY.

Modesty is a polite accomplishment, and generally attendant upon merit. It is engaging, in the highest degree, and wins the hearts of all with whom we are acquainted. None are more disgusting in company, than the impudent and presuming.

Nothing can atone for the

want of modesty; without it, beauty is ungraceful, and wit detestable.

Be particularly careful not to speak of yourself, if you can help it. An impudent person intrudes himself abruptly upon all occasions, and is ever the hero of his own story.

The less you say of yourself, the more the world will

give you credit for; and the more you say of yourself, the less they will believe you.

Whatever perfections you may have, be assured people will find them out; but whether they do or not, nobody will take them upon your own word.

CIVILITY.

The art of pleasing is a very necessary one to possess, but a very difficult one to acquire. It can hardly be reduced to rules, and your own good sense and observation will teach you more of it than I can. Do as you would be done by, is the surest method of pleasing.

Observe carefully what is pleasing to you in others; and probably the same things in you will please others.

If you are pleased with the complaisance and attention of others to you, depend upon it, the same complaisance and attention, on your part, will equally please them.

It is not enough not to be rude; you should be civil and

distinguished for your good breeding. The first principle of this good breeding is, never to say anything that you think can be disagreeable to anybody in company; but, on the contrary, you should endeavor to say what will be agreeable to them; and that in an easy and natural manner, without seeming to study for compliments. There is likewise such a thing as a civil look and a rude look; you should look civil, as well as be so; for if, while you are saying a civil thing, you look gruff and surly, nobody will be obliged to you for a civility that seemed to come so unwillingly.

If you have occasion to contradict any one, or to set him right from a mistake, it would be very brutal to say,

"That is not so; I know better;" or, "You are wrong;" but you should say, with a civil look, "I beg your pardon, I believe you mistake;" or, "If I may take the liberty of contradicting you, I believe it is so and so:" for, though you may know a thing better than other people, yet is very disagreeable to tell them so, directly, without something to soften it; but remember particularly, that whatever you may say or do, with ever so civil an intention, a great deal consists in the manner and the look, which must be genteel, easy, and natural.

Civility is particularly due to all women; and remember that no provocation whatever can justify any person in being uncivil to a woman; and the greatest man in the land would be reckoned a brute, if he was not civil to the meanest woman. It is due to their sex, and is the only protection they have against the superior strength of ours.

MORAL CHARACTER.

There is nothing so delicate as your moral character, and nothing that it is your interest so much to preserve pure. Should you be suspected of injustice, malignity, perfidy, lying, &c., all the parts and knowledge in the world will never procure you esteem, friendship, or respect. A strange concurrence of circumstances has sometimes raised very bad men to high stations; but they have been raised, like criminals to a pillory, where their persons and their crimes, by being more conspicuous, are only the more known, the more pelted and insulted. If in any case whatsoever, dissimulation were pardonable, it would be in the case of morality; though, even then, a Pharasaical pomp of virtue would not be advisable. But I will recommend to you a most scrupulous tenderness for your moral character, and the utmost care not to do or say anything that may ever so slightly taint it. Show yourself, upon all occasions, the advocate, the friend, but not the bully, of virtue.

GOOD BREEDING.

Observe the best and most well-bred of the French people; how agreeably they insinuate little civilities in their conversation. They think it so essential that they call an honest and a civil man by the same name, of "honnete homme;" and the Romans called civility, "humanitas," as thinking it inseparable from humanity: and depend upon it, that your reputation and success will, in a great measure, depend upon the degree of good breeding of which you are master.

From what has been said, I conclude with the observation, that gentleness of manners, with firmness of mind, is a short but full description of human perfection, on this side of religious and moral duties.

www.ingramcontent.com/pod-product-compliance
Lightning Source LLC
Chambersburg PA
CBHW021134300426
44113CB00006B/422